Black-Footed Country

Black-Footed

Country

Poems by Lindsay Wilson

Liquid Light Press

Premium Chapbook First Edition

Copyright © 2015 by Lindsay Wilson

ISBN-10: 0990926729

ISBN-13: 978-0-9909267-2-6

Liquid Light Press

poetry that speaks to the heart

www.liquidlightpress.com

Cover Photo by Harry Wilson
(*www.harrywilsonphoto.com*)

Photo of Poet by Anna Wilson

Cover Design by M. D. Friedman
(*www.mdfriedman.com*)

Who but a poet would want death reading over his shoulder?

—Juan Ramón Jiménez

Contents

Mother Seen as a Dress on a Line 1

No Elegies 3

Mother, ... 6

Ars Poetica 7

Long Division 9

The Day's Other Face 11

Surrender, A Prayer for my Mother 13

A Few Theories on Starlings and Dandelions 14

Elegy with Lawn Gnome 16

Mother, ... 18

The Night I Woke Up and Didn't See the Neighborhood Burning Down 19

Black-Footed Country 21

Mother, ... 22

What Memory Wants 23

Elegy with no Shotgun 25

No Revision 28

Christmas Eve 2011 After Taking Yu Troung to Radiation, Christmas Eve
2012 After Learning He Passed 31

About the Author 35

Acknowledgements and Credits 37

Mother Seen as a Dress on a Line

After so many summers of fire you found
yourself complaining all through a green July,

and by the time you flipped the calendar's page,
you're deep into a late August day

walking the dog between the freckles of low
pines when you both hear the owl's song,

a call without a body, carrying across
the creosote field from the other side

of the dry canal where someone
in the distance beats a rug hung from a line,

and with each swing something old rises
briefly into the air, dust in back lit sun

curling and drifting in a twisting wind
that distorts and billows, at the end of the line,

a long white dress into a body, into something
almost human, and you understand this is your first

heated projection into the distance. At home
the phone's ringing. It's been ringing all day,

and you're the only child, the only teller
who walks now with your mind wrestling

with the dress filling and lifting for the wind.
The world's calling. Everyone wants to know

the Story of How. So how does it feel,
this life, this evening walk with a tired dog

up a dry hill, knowing that as of today,
there's no longer a woman to call, *Mother?*

No Elegies

Your therapist banned the word elegy
from your notebooks, by therapist I mean

the woman who runs your poetry workshop
at the food court in the high-end fashion mall

where apparently no one dies. Elegy is so,
what's the year Levis passed? Yeah, then.

No one said the sale would last forever,
and anyway, lately, haven't you been confusing

your favorite literary magazines for sales
catalogs? Doesn't your therapist say,

You shouldn't make everything into a poem.
Usually you're halfway up the drive before

you realize you're reading ad copy instead
of a haiku sequence. Haiku? Who do you

think you are? Basho? Hass? McGrath?
No, you're the odd boy standing

in your kitchen gazing out the window
where the whole world's a giant no.

The beautiful daisies half in fence shadow?
Old fashioned. The stark morning moon?

Are you being ironic? Your father's old
push mower leaning against a wall? A tool

from another century. You can't help loving
the transience. The waning moon. The flowers

that only love for a season. The rust dulling
the blades. Don't you love the Once of back-story,

or objects suddenly aglow, lit from within
by the human gaze? You were the boy who knew

all the lyrics from your parents' old records,
and you settled didn't you? Settled

for the high school English gig full of missed allegory,
settled for Saturdays spent in the food court

where your therapist puzzles and moans over
your new poem's ending: Once you stood before

the turned earth of the dead, and you thought
it the shape of a door, but without a handle,

so how do you enter without a lock to pick?
At lunch on the patio, a man pulled a dove

from his sleeve, and he let you touch it to make
it real for everyone else, and in one toss you saw

the bird become action, become flight,
and in that just-past-your-reach moment

your father said, *Don't worry. He's trained
to fly back to his cage.* Like a heart, you thought,

but said, *Don't ruin it.* You felt defiant in your grief.
At least then you could tell the world, as it drifted

below you, how you felt, how you could feel your hollow
boned lightness, how you could feel the hinges

of your wings pivot on the wind.

Mother,

I'm tired of reading
the signs like a neighbor
balancing the weight
of three newspapers
on the drive,

                tired
of the way the plant's
dry soil tells him how long
it's been kept from water.

Bakersfield now is always August
with its wide open mouth trying
to get everything inside:

all those aphids devouring
the roses and the tarantula
wasps, like the past, trying
to put the weight of its eggs
in our backs.

                There are too
many things for our gaze
to fall upon, and misread
like a sign, so I've packed
up the car and written
this note, but now

I don't know where
it should be sent.

Ars Poetica

When the police broke through the backdoor,
the window fell in pieces like the start of a story,

something in the middle of things, or already
at the end, depending on how the pieces are picked up

and arranged. Either way they must be gathered,
this trail of crumbed glass, this crumbled line

from backdoor to the back bedroom, this path the police
took to her body past the restored radio her father

cobbled together from the parts of old radios
no one ever listens to anymore, those radios

that must warm up before telling their who-done-its,
that refinished wood hiding the tubes inside.

The tubes, she told her son as a child, still held
the voices of the past, something trapped,

and if he could tune it just so, there they suddenly
were, almost alive and speaking to him on his knees,

squinting his ears at the needle, hand on the knob.
But he's no child now trying to hear those old voices,

there's no nothing dead-alive in those tubes
despite all the antique frequencies no one listens

to anymore, not even the police, not even him,
or the coroner who followed the glass to her,

who took note of how she broke her nose, falling
in her last steps, the small halo there of dried blood,

the temperature of the body, how she knelt
over her and slipped from a finger her wedding ring

to place in the jewelry case by the antique Czech
glass earrings he bought her. He gave the band

to his stepfather, gave the earrings to his fiancée,
and when he gathered the broken glass on the carpet,

it was almost beautiful, almost something to be hung
from sterling silver, then an ear, beautiful there to catch

the light for his eyes so it would lead back to what hears
his story. Her listening. Her ears adorned

with the antique glass she always wore when she knew
his eyes and her would be meeting.

Long Division

Death divides us into those who can clean
the blood stains of family and those who cannot.

The coroner called it pooling, normal,
this dark troubled-spot by her bed,

but I named it place of her last misstep, thought,
and had no desire to clean it. For days

I walked past it, stepping over its threshold
as I entered the room to part the blackout

curtains covering the glass door to the patio,
but the light never seemed long enough

to reach it, wash it — even in the length
of evening it could not touch it. I took out

my measuring tape, a pencil, a small notebook,
a matter of inches. I thought perhaps

during one of June's long days the sun
could make it. I had plans, calendars

and almanacs, though, I always fail
at forethought and math, but on that shrinking

late September day, the sun stopped two
and a quarter inches from her blood. I know.

I measured twice. When I stretched out
next to it, almost my whole body aglow

in dusk-light, all the dead relatives
from their pictures seemed to watch.

I memorized the ages of all of them,
then divided by the distance between frames,

added the baby nephew before I subtracted
all the Baptist family in Dallas, and I understood

this is where it ends, Mother, alone and blue-lipped
on the stained carpet as the gathered dead

look down on us with all of those unblinking
eyes, all those still mouths, and that carefully

measured distance between us shrinking.

The Day's Other Face

Because you haven't stopped in weeks
you still feel the constant rattle of road,

and even at dusk, when you finally try
to stop for the night's first beer

like your mother walking in from work
to pour that first glass of wine. No music.

No television. No talking, she'd say
as she sat staring off into nothing

and began to wrestle with whatever
of the day's voices she still had to reconcile

in her mind before the evening could roll over
to show her other face. Today you desire

anything you think will stop the questions,
but you cannot shake the road's thrum

from your bones, and you understand
you're praying for the first time. How dramatically

stupid you feel in your bartering, your shaky
hands empty with nothing to offer,

but you find here a sort of relief,
and then the lamp by her ashes casts

its sudden spell of light into the dusky room,
and this rattled moment feels like a torch

dropping through some deep well before
going out, and you remember you

put the lamp on a timer, so it would look
like someone was here when no one was home.

Surrender, A Prayer for my Mother

Listen, dark one, as the sun sets,

the boxelder beetles come down
from the west wall to fly back

to their nymph tree, and in this late light

the long ash leaves look like the points
of bronze spears, dark and bloody

with the busy blush of the beetles' scarlet

wings. After the sun falls below
the Sierras, and the sundial becomes

useless under these lengthening shadows,

the fine-armed daughters of night
will sever your tether to this dim world,

then, dark one, you will no longer

be bound to this place. You will lay
down your spears. You will find

your red-black wings.

A Few Theories on Starlings and Dandelions

The dead spill and drift into the mold-black
earth and tug on the curtain of loss

as the wind stirs their ash-dust into a fist
that unclenches like a dandelion letting go

of its seeds. I have a theory about seeds
and loss and the small birds I've introduced

to live off both. I have theories I try
to forget about dandelions, words

and memories I try to pull out whole,
taproot and all. I have theories about herbicide

and the cultivation of non-native species
to eat the dead. I have knelt on the earth

with a trowel and let my digging say,
Don't come back. My theories aren't prayers,

aren't small birds with their low trajectories,
hunger and warbled-faulty song. The dead

have their mouths of ash, their flower-seeds,
the jagged tooth leaves of dandelions

that always come back waving their goddamn
yellow flags. I have a theory about growth,

about the color yellow, about the hair
and fingernails of the dead still inching out

past the moment of reaching. Are you a body?
Are you ash? Are you a box, a box of ash,

opened and spread thin and merging
with the earth like a seed taking its first step

to root, to growing under my skin like a song
I don't want to know the words for? And yet

I'm digging in, I'm singing hopelessly along.

Elegy with Lawn Gnome

Something grows under my grass at night,
poking its white caps out from the earth

in a fairy ring. In the window above it sits
the ashes of a woman I cannot bury,

and since she has lost her eyes
I hide a cracked, faded lawn gnome

leaning on a toadstool between the wild roses
tell him to report to me each morning,

but he just says, *cottontail.* He says, *blue jay.*
He says, *nothing.* That's all he ever says,

and I confess I put those words in his mouth
because that's what I do when someone dies,

put my words into things, then ask them to speak
for me, though, I don't want my words.

I want a new name for understanding,
more phrases for something lost.

My gardener names the ring's bare earth center
the dead zone. *But the dead zone,* I say,

keeps growing like the swells of a blue stone
dropped into a pond, and the gnome and I

are tired of the dead growing in our yard.
The gardener doesn't trust the gnome,

but tells me even the dead zone eventually dies.
At dusk the gnome and I drink a few beers

while staring at the hole in our lawn
where grass should be. *I'm sorry,* I say,

for putting my words in your mouth, sorry
for my inheritance of fungus, these white caps

like toes exposed from a shallow grave.

Mother,

You did not need an invitation
to appear on the sidewalk at dusk,

so I took you out of my loss

and crushed you with the thistles
from the burned field then spread
across the doorways of my house.

Now, afraid to leave, I wander
the rooms asking the mirrors
if they too own a memory
of your reflection.
            They, like you,
stay silent.
         When the thunder speaks,
I open the windows to the hot house
and notice,
        for the first time,

how the backlit Sierras look
like a jagged cardiac line
pulsing against the horizon
before flat lining into the Great Basin,

and there you are again, outside
looking in, hand pressed to the screen

while the wind and rain pass through
a body that isn't there.

The Night I Woke Up and Didn't See
the Neighborhood Burning Down

I understood you passed down your insomnia
after weeks of waking during the dead hour,

but sadness had snuck up behind me to place
its hands over my eyes. Had I opened my blinds

I would have noticed a world domed in a dark
orange glow, a tangle of flames up the hill,

and so blindness taught me its advantages
as I cupped water to my face, then studied

on my elm-skin hands my frayed and forked
lifeline that you carved into my palms,

mother, which is something like an inheritance,
this wooden myopia of self, all those leaves

I grew to cover my eyes. Soon I found
sleep, and the next day I awoke to a landscape

layered in ash, though, the night before
unknown to me, just blocks away, fathers woke

their kids from the smoky darkness of sleep,
placed them wrapped in the backseat, and once

they saw everyone was there, the mothers began
the old stories of flight, which always start

with smoke rising from under the door
as the hands of someone we love pulls us

out of ourselves to push us into a new world
where the rain drifting into our eyes is ash.

Black-Footed Country

I proposed fire as another form of growth
the morning we woke to find the field of sage

and creosote replaced by wind-stoked smoke
and burning bushes. My mother had recently passed,

so you thought I was speaking in metaphor,
but I said I was speaking in world. That evening

the clouds wrung from our hopes appeared
and rained the ash from the air, and I came back

to my mourning in this new black-footed
country where I still couldn't write that grief,

and yet I knew some dormant seeds need fire to grow.
Another metaphor, you said, *What do you want?*

I asked, *The smell of creosote after a desert rain?*
Can't have that, you said. *They were all consumed.*

So I wrote of the steam rising from the charcoal fields,
and how lost I felt watching the returned-evacuated

children's flashlights scatter across the ridgeline,
and in between their shrieks of laughter I thought,

Where are the mothers to lead them home?

Mother,

Today I rise early to walk
the dog along the river,

restless and looking for what
the world will give: half-filled jar

of salmon eggs, broken antler,
a tripwire fishing line I pull up

and follow to a landlocked pool,
filled by a spring flood, then abandoned,

destined, by early summer, to dry up.
At the sound of my feet a school

of minnows startles out of their stillness,
and when I drop in a pink egg, they return

like my grief under the netted shadows
of the cottonwoods, exposed

in their appetite. I am training
my grief to rise from the shallows

for each bright egg, but even after
the jar empties, all those little mouths

still blindly bite at the surface.

What Memory Wants

The moths, those little white flames
of evening, have grown tired of beating

their chapped wings against the street lights,
and have silenced themselves into the leaves

along your porch where this morning,
in my sleeplessness, I imagine you robed,

kneeling down to clip rosemary
to bake later with chicken and the juice

of two lemons already resting on the table
with your coffee. Mother, did you notice

the new owner removed the shrubs
we planted along the fence line and dug up

the succulents from the porch's shade?
Mother, we showed him the room in which

you passed, and too early I am awake
with the guilt of selling that ground

because if the importance of place
are the acts committed to memory there,

then I am ashamed this morning has pressed
the gold coins of nostalgia to my palms

letting me see you in the kitchen,
garlic and rosemary on the counter

and you juicing a lemon while the flames
of yellow finches darting from your wrists

and into memory's want, rise into the high branches
to grow fat like a sour fruit, and remain far

from our reach where they belong.

Elegy with no Shotgun

After everyone left me alone in her house,
I searched her closet first filled with sundresses
the smell of old, floral perfume,

then mine, empty and dusty for years,
and the guest bedroom and the next,
through the hallway closets and into the garage

with its corners filled with boxes and tools,
but still no gun oil, no wooden handle.
Not even in the black widow shed

could I find my old 410 overlay,
but finally beside the lawn mower
with its litter of dry, cut grass, I cleared away

a space in my mind and remembered
after her last failed suicide my father,
her long-ago ex, whose custody the state

so embarrassingly placed her in,
had taken it with others to be destroyed.
The gravel floor crunched like gritting teeth

as I ran to her car and sped off into the Sierra
foothills for any road to announce itself,
to say left here, right there. What the fuck

did direction matter? I wanted speed
under me. I needed a dirt road, more gravel
and a sun to come down hard on every damn thing

at some dead end. Some failed oil field lease.
Some collapsed homestead. Some place
to be in the world's teeth and chewed

until screaming took me, until only shooting
would do for the I-want-holes-in-everything mood
I was in. What do you give such hungry

and empty hands? So you've heard
this story. So your cynicism eats at you
like the bullet holes rusting through this fallen,

corrugated roof. Say, so what. Say who cares.
Say death sleeps in everyone's bed.
What is it to you that once, as a boy,

I shot at clay pigeons and the ground
broke every one? So she took me out from under
the gaze of the men who laughed

with each of my shots. Quail sprung from sage,
ran through the red rocks, and vanished
into the yellow bloom of rabbit brush.

She said, *easy, relax.* She said, *try again.*
But my anger swelled with everything I missed.
Once there was patience, a mother and son

alone, and the perfect complete arch of clay pigeons
that must break when finally their flight
takes them back to this hard, dry earth.

No Revision

This evening, as a tiding of magpies perch too loudly
in the low pines, I reread the last pages from the history book

of the correspondence between my mother and I, my fifth
beer sweating onto my grandfather's oak table. If you read

this scrapbook of knee-jerk letters and cards glued to the pages,
some blank, some torn out, you'd find at the end the first draft

of Bishop's "One Art" next to the final draft that I sent
after a woman my mother knew insisted, *You cannot revise*

poetry. It's too personal. She called too late that night,
and in between gulps of wine, I heard her familiar near manic

voice, the long pauses as she measured each syllable,
each nuance of word before speaking too carefully,

before finally saying, exasperated, *Isn't that crazy?*
Tonight, I've winched up her manic voice into the trees

to let it carry between the two poles of me, east to west.
The magpies, their calls sharp and angry, now fight

in the road over a truck-hit coyote. My bird dog whines
at the fence line. *No, you're not crazy, Mother,* I wrote

on the drafts of Bishop's poem before sending my last note.
The day she died, I spoke with the coroner on the phone

about her depression, suicide attempts, and Lupus' beak
picking at her old heart. She asked, *Would your stepfather?*

No, I said. And then suddenly she said, *What do you do?*
I try to teach writing. She asked, *You recently sent poems?*

And I saw her in my mother's room, this lady whose job
deals with the art of losing daily. They had already

carried my mother out under the feathered shadows
of trees and inside the coroner read "One Art" thinking,

No, shit. The art of losing isn't hard to master.
On the road, the magpies pick from the coyote's torn stomach,

and so scavenger eats scavenger, and the entrails spill out,
pulled from beak to bloody beak, then they carve their jagged

lines across the liver. Lines I read later, my dog straining
at her leash as the birds screech from the bouldered hill.

I can't predict the future. I can't read the scars on my liver.
I don't know what long history the coroner found inside her,

but I wanted to tell her how terribly we ended, still fighting
over my name on a failed suicide note without apology

and no way now to revise. I wanted to know what the coroner
found when she read the lines scarring her liver. Did she discover

I was an awful son? Maybe some things are too personal.
Maybe language never means what we desire so revising

is meaningless, and in some wrong way that lady was right.
But what do I know? I only revise my words on the page

and never my life. Maybe the coroner sat there flipping
between the first and final drafts thinking about the day's

new loss, and understood, for the first time, the art of losing
is hard to master. Tonight that thought lifts like a tiding

of black and white birds rising from a boulder strewn hillside,
and for a second they hold there, blocking out a few early stars,

and revise the bright blemishes from the evening sky.

Christmas Eve 2011 After Taking Yu Troung to Radiation, Christmas Eve 2012 After Learning He Passed

The worst thing about death must be the first night.
—— Juan Ramón Jiménez

Snow drifts through the dark
then porch light before settling

into the bucket I used to mix soil
with manure to spread with seed

across my lawn where now snow grows,
flake by flake, slowly the way

a blues song enters us note by note,
or the way I imagine radiation

entered your body drip by accumulating
drip until your body said enough,

and on the drive home you gave it all
back to the bucket you kept at your feet

then carried to the porch to set down
like an afterthought, though, I never

wanted you to become an afterthought,
a bucket your wife hosed out, something

we used to beat like a drum
to keep us in time. Later it filled

with the accumulation of sprinkler and rain,
and I had a thought then I let pass,

an image really, of you on your porch
late that night, sleepless as I am now,

pencil in hand, harmonica in yours,
and when you peered down into the reflection

of your thin, sunken face did you see
our mothers looking down from their dark

windows above us telling us to sleep?
Because I can't. Though I know tonight

when the snow comes down like a curtain
on the sky, it means the moment

for all of those afterthoughts has passed,
it means it's time to play, to hold those notes

you love most rough and ragged
in your mouth because you'll have to sing

yourself to sleep, you'll have to practice
to turn your body into song.

About the Author

Lindsay Wilson, an English professor at Truckee Meadows Community College, has been a finalist for the Philip Levine Prize, and he has published five chapbooks. His first book, *No Elegies*, won the Quercus Review Press Spring Book Award 2014. He co-edits the literary and arts journal, *The Meadow*, and his poetry has appeared in *The Minnesota Review, Verse Daily, The Portland Review, Pank,* and *The Bellevue Literary Review,* among others.

Acknowledgements and Credits

"A Few Theories on Starlings and Dandelions" was published in *Compose*.

"Black-Footed Country" was published in the *Minnesota Review*.

"Elegy with no Shotgun" was published by the *New Plains Review*.

"Christmas Eve 2011 After Taking Yu Troung to Radiation, Christmas Eve 2012 After Learning He Passed" was published in the *Naugatuck River Review*.

"Mother, You did not need..." was published in the *Cumberland River Review*.

"Surrender, A Prayer for my Mother" was published in the *Bellevue Literary Review*.

"Mother, Today I rise early..." was published in *Sundog Lit*.

"Mother Seen as Dress on a Line" and "Elegy with Lawn Gnome" are forthcoming in *Clerestory*.

Other Books from Liquid Light Press

All Liquid Light Press books are available directly from *liquidlightpress.com* or from any of the current major global distribution channels including Amazon, Barnes and Noble, the iBookstore and the Ingram Catalog.

Leaning Toward Whole, **Poems by M. D. Friedman (Released June, 2011)**
This poetry chapbook from the international award winning poet, M. D. Friedman, contains pieces both poignant and personal.

The Miracle Already Happening – Everyday Life with Rumi, **Poems by Rosemerry Wahtola Trommer (Released December, 2011)**
Rosemerry Wahtola Trommer's superb collection of poems, inspired by Rumi, is full of heart, humor, peace and wisdom.

Spiral, **Poems by Lynda La Rocca (Released March, 2012)**
Award winning poet, Lynda La Rocca, creates a compelling poetic and melodic discourse from the persistent cravings and fears inside of each of us.

From the Ashes, **Poems by Wayne A. Gilbert (Released June , 2012)**
From the Ashes is a true masterpiece that gnaws at the heart with universal appeal.

ah, **Poems by Rachel Kellum (Released July, 2012)**
Rachel Kellum's poetry has a simplicity and clarity that cuts to the core of being human.

Catalyst, **Poems by Jeremy Martin (Released December, 2012)**
Catalyst may just launch you on a fiery ride into yourself.

Of Eyes and Iris, **Poems by Erika Moss Gordon (Released March, 2013)**
Beautiful yet poignant in its simplicity, *Of Eyes and Iris,* will call you back again and again for another read.

Your House Is Floating, **Poems by Susan Whitmore (Released June, 2013)**
Susan Whitmore's craft is as smooth, crisp and satisfying as olive oil on fresh garden greens.

Nowhere Near Morning, **Poems by Jeffrey M. Bernstein (Released October, 2013)**
Nowhere Near Morning is an intimate embrace of what it means to be alive, a wakeup call for those falling asleep at the wheel of their daily grind.

Harmonica, **Poems by Cecele Allen Kraus (Released March, 2014)**
Harmonica bristles with a shimmering music that heals the heart.

Surf Sounds, **Poems by Roger Higgins (Released October 2014)**
Expertly crafted and elegantly written, you will return often to these poetic beaches pulsing with insightful breezes and the tides of the heart.

www.ingramcontent.com/pod-product-compliance
Lightning Source LLC
Chambersburg PA
CBHW021915040426
42447CB00007B/867